BEAR LEARNS HOW TO BE A FISH

Deirdre Brandner and Jennifer Whelan

Published by Wilkinson Publishing Pty Ltd
ACN 006 042 173
PO Box 24135, Melbourne, VIC 3001, Australia
Ph: +61 3 9654 5446
enquiries@wilkinsonpublishing.com.au
www.wilkinsonpublishing.com.au

© Copyright Deirdre Brandner and Jennifer Whelan 2024

All rights reserved. No part of this publication may be reproduced, stored in a retrieval system or transmitted in any form by any means without the prior permission of the copyright owner. Enquiries should be made to the publisher.

Every effort has been made to ensure that this book is free from error or omissions. However, the Publisher, the Authors, the Editor or their respective employees or agents, shall not accept responsibility for injury, loss or damage occasioned to any person acting or refraining from action as a result of material in this book whether or not such injury, loss or damage is in any way due to any negligent act or omission, breach of duty or default on the part of the Publisher, the Authors, the Editor, or their respective employees or agents.

ISBN: 9781922810632

A catalogue record for this book is available from the National Library of Australia.

Illustrations by Jennifer Whelan
Design by Tango Media
Printed and bound in China

Follow Wilkinson Publishing on social media.

 WilkinsonPublishing

 wilkinsonpublishinghouse

 WPBooks

Bear stood by the pond.
'I am worried,' Bear said to the fish.
'I am too scared to cross to the other side
of the pond to get my favorite treat…
a honey chocolate milkshake!
Bear pointed his honey straw toward
the other side of the water.

'You have a boat,' said the fish.
'That will get you safely across the pond.'

'No,' said Bear. 'I am very worried. What if my boat bumps into a whale before I reach the other side?'

'Hmm…' said the fish.
'I haven't seen a whale in this pond before.
I don't think whales live in ponds.'

'I am still worried,' Bear said to the fish.
'What if it rains and my boat fills up with water?
My boat will sink before I reach the other side.

'Hmm…' said the fish.
'There are no clouds in the sky.
Should it happen to rain, I see you have
a very large umbrella.
That will keep your boat from filling with water.'

'I am still worried,' Bear said to the fish.
'What if I get ants in my pants?
My boat will tip upside down as
I'm jumping to shake out the ants.

I will never reach the other side of the pond.
I will never get my honey chocolate milkshake.'

'Hmm…' said the fish.
'I see your pants fit you well
and it would be hard for ants
to find a way in.

But if you do get ants in your pants,
you could sit down with a heavy thud.
Ants do not like being sat on
and they don't know how to swim.'

You worry a lot,' said the fish.
'When I get worried I take a BIG breath in and

slowly breathe out

I swim through all of my bubbles.
It helps me not to worry should I bump into a shark,
even though I don't think sharks live in ponds.'

The fish swam away breathing out lots of bubbles.

So Bear imagined he was a fish.
He picked up his honey straw.
He took a BIG breath in then...

Slowly breathed out

And he thought of how
many honey chocolate milkshake
bubbles such a big breath could make.

Bear then got into his boat with his very large umbrella and his honey straw.
He sailed across the water to the other side of the pond to get a honey chocolate milkshake.

Then Bear's boat went
BUMP!

Bear began to worry...
Had his boat bumped into
a giant whale?

So Bear imagined he was a fish.
He picked up his honey straw.
He took a BIG breath in then...

Slowly breathed out

And he thought of how many honey chocolate milkshake bubbles such a big breath could make.

Bear was no longer worried.
His boat had only bumped into a very large rock.
There was not a whale in sight.

Bear sailed further across the pond
and was almost halfway to the other side.
Then suddenly dark clouds filled the sky
and it started raining. Bear opened up his umbrella.

Bear worried that his boat would fill with water and would sink all the way to the bottom of the pond.

So Bear imagined he was a fish.
He picked up his honey straw.
He took a BIG breath in then...

Slowly breathed out

And he thought of how
many honey chocolate milkshake
bubbles such a big breath could make.

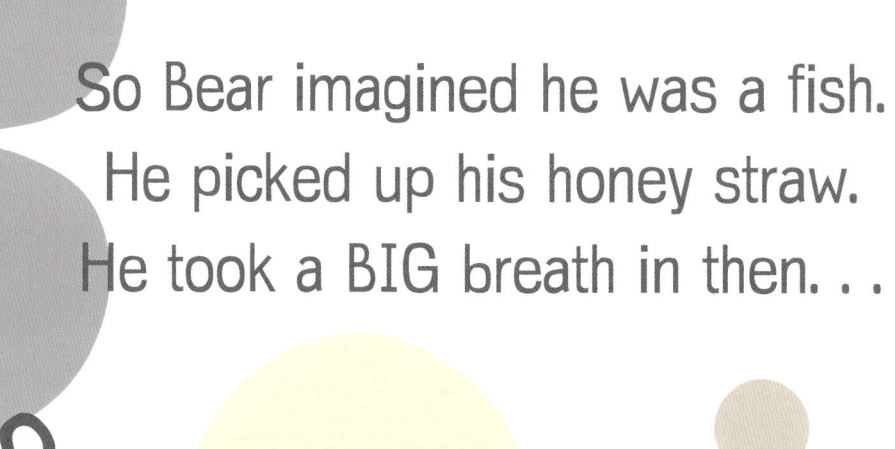

Bear no longer felt worried.
The rain stopped and Bear's boat
was as dry as could be.

Bear was almost to the other side of the pond.

Then suddenly Bear's pants started itching and twitching. Bear worried he had ants in his pants. He started jumping about. The boat was sure to tip upside down.

So Bear imagined he was a fish.
He picked up his honey straw.
He took a BIG breath in then...

Slowly breathed out

And he thought of how
many honey chocolate milkshake
bubbles such a big breath could make.

Bear no longer felt worried.
He sat down with a thud.
He stopped itching and twitching
and there wasn't an ant in sight.

Bear finally reached the other side of the pond...

And he got a BIG honey chocolate milkshake.

Now, whenever Bear gets worried,
he knows how to be a fish.

Bear's Toolkit

Worry thinking can trick us into believing the very worst. Worry thinking comes with lots of yucky feelings that trick us into thinking that these thoughts are true.

These tools will help you and your child manage those tricky thoughts and identify the logical thoughts.

With your child, compare Bear's worry thinking and Fish's ideas.

Was Bear's worrying thinking logical?
What happens when you have a worry thought?
Is your worry thinking trying to trick you?
Does it try and make you feel yucky?

Let's practice saying our worry thoughts and talk back with logical thoughts, just like Fish does.

"Mum won't know where to pick me up."

Fish would help you talk back to your worry and say,
"Doesn't your mum pick you up everyday? "

For really annoying worries, we write down
some ways to fix tricky situations. We can
have a plan. Worries hate plans.

"What if the work at school is too hard?"
Let's think… what would be a plan?
Maybe you could have a go, and think
it's okay to make a mistake.
Maybe you could see how others are doing the work.
Maybe you could ask your friend to help.
Maybe you could ask your teacher for help.

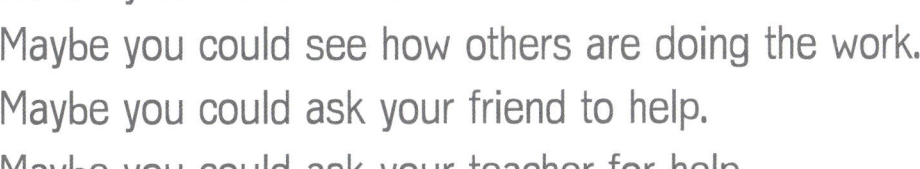

Practice Honey Milkshake Breathing with your straw. You might like to do this in your milkshake and then you can see how many gentle bubbles you can make with one long breath. Take a deep breath in and blow gently and slowly out. Don't let the bubbles spill.

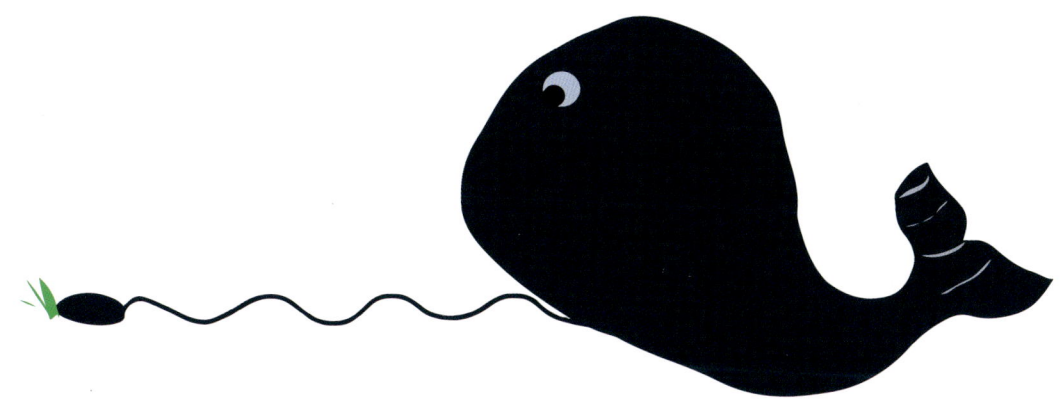

Choose what size your worry thought is: Pebble Size or a Whale Size. Talk with someone about making it smaller.

 **Jennifer Whelan** is an author, an illustrator an expert bubble maker. Whenever she worries whether her boat might bump into a whale, she takes a deep breath in and slowly breathes out and just like Bear she imagines how many honey chocolate milkshake bubbles she can make.

To all the whale size worries of the world… POP!

 **Deirdre Brandner** is a psychologist with over 30 years experience supporting children and adolescents in the areas of Anxiety and Autism spectrum. Deirdre provides evidence based techniques in Bear's Toolkit that will help young readers recognise their worries, and use the calming tools to manage fear and overthinking with strategies that help manage anxiety and build resilience.